VIRAT KOHLI

Reliable Rebel

VIRAT KOHLI

Reliable Rebel

AYAZ MEMON

by
C Rajshekar Rao

JAICO PUBLISHING HOUSE

Ahmedabad Bangalore Bhopal Bhubaneswar Chennai
Delhi Hyderabad Kolkata Lucknow Mumbai

Published by Jaico Publishing House
A-2 Jash Chambers, 7-A Sir Phirozshah Mehta Road
Fort, Mumbai - 400 001
jaicopub@jaicobooks.com
www.jaicobooks.com

VIRAT KOHLI
ISBN 978-81-8495-524-8

First Jaico Impression: 2014
Fifth Jaico Impression: 2017

Printed by
Repro India Limited
Plot No. 50/2, T.T.C. MIDC Industrial Area
Mahape, Navi Mumbai - 400 710

Contents

Contents

Publisher's Foreword

Cricket has always been a compelling addiction in India. But the recent past has seen a massive explosion in the game's reach, its audience and money. As a result, cricketers now compete with film stars in adoration quotient and quite often, win that battle.

With the spread of the Indian diaspora, cricket is now watched in more countries than it is played in. Cricket's ascendancy has also sparked a tremendous demand for information, where fans devour every last tidbit they can about their favourite players.

To these aficionados, Jaico Publishing House is delighted to present, with Ayaz Memon as editor, the Cricketwallah Series — a set of books that contain information, comment, statistics and much more about some of India's most admired and followed cricketers. These books are written with zest for a quick read and then to treasure, for future reference.

Ayaz Memon is India's best known sports writer with over 35 years in journalism. He has covered more Tests and tournaments than he can remember, as well as the Olympic Games, Wimbledon and more. He has authored several books over his long and illustrious career and has been a cricket commentator, in both English and Hindi, for television channels.

There is near unanimous consensus amongst expeerts that Virat Kohli is the best batsman in the world in his age group and I see no reason to disagree. His prolific form – in all formats – over the past couple of years only corroborates such estimation.

Over the last two years, he has been supremely consistent in his run-making in Tests, One-Day Internationals and T20 formats. In limited overs cricket particularly, Kohli has been in the forefront in India's rise to eminence again after a disappointing run post the 2011 World Cup victory.

In ODIs particularly, he is touching greatness with 15 centuries already to his credit in just 113 matches and a batting average which is just a shade under 50 which puts him alongside former maestros like Viv Richards, Sachin Tendulkar and Ricky Ponting to name a few.

Obviously Kohli will have to sustain this form for at least a decade longer to retain comparison with the names mentioned above and he has given every indication that he intends to do that. His love for cricket is evident, he loves to compete, loves to win and loves the attention and rewards that success has brought him.

Ever since he led India to victory in the under-19 World Cup in 2008, Kohli was identified as a future star and captain. In the five years since, he hit a rocky patch for a while, losing his equanimity and focus in the first flush of fame he received, but recovered in time to live up to his early promise.

He does not have a copybook technique, what with a dominant bottom hand. But he has shown the intelligence and adaptability to succeed at the highest level. Most important perhaps is his mental toughness. He does not fear any opponent or situation: in fact, he revels in a crisis.

Kohli has cemented his place in the Test team on the back of several crucial knocks in the 2012-13 season and is arguably now the most resourceful Indian cricketer in every format after Mahendra Singh Dhoni. As a part time bowler he can be relied on to break partnerships. Add to that his brilliant fielding and his value is enhanced manifold.

Even as a youngster he showed strong leadership qualities and is now tipped to take over the captaincy from Dhoni. In the few opportunities that he has got yet to lead the team, he has shown a good grip over tactics and fellow-player motivation.

There were some critics who thought Kohli's overt aggression would work against a convivial dressing room apart from rubbing opponents and others the wrong way. But he has matured rapidly without compromising on playing the game hard.

Only 25, Kohli is a vibrant metaphor of an India team that has undergone a makeover in the past couple of years. His youthfulness, energy and ambition define the New Age Indian cricketer. He can be brash, but he also knows that it's performance, not theatrics, which ultimately matter.

In this book, Delhi journalist C Rajshekhar Rao, who has seen and reported on Virat Kohli for the past decade, traces his rise to eminence through trials and tribulations and tells us what makes the young cricketer such a dynamic force in the game today.

AYAZ MEMON
October 15, 2013
Mumbai

Career Highlights

- 2008: Virat Kohli captained the Indian team that won the ICC Under-19 Cricket World Cup

- January 2012: In the Perth Test against Australia, Kohli made 44 and 75 runs to become the third youngest Indian to top score in both innings of a Test, after Sunil Gavaskar and Lala Amarnath

- For three consecutive calendar years (2010, 2011, 2012), Kohli has been India's leading run-scorer in ODIs, with 995, 1381 and 1026 runs respectively

- Kohli has a batting average of 60.72 in chases in ODIs as against his career average of 49.72

- Nine of Kohli's 15 ODI hundreds have come in the chases. India won all of them!

- Kohli is the quickest among Indians to reach the milestone of 1000 runs, 3000 runs and 4000 runs in ODIs

- Kohli is the youngest to score 15 ODI centuries. He reached the milestone at the age of 24 years, 261 days. He has also taken the least innings (106) to do so

Compiled by Rajnish Gupta

1

CHAPTER

IN A LITTLE LEAGUE
OF HIS OWN

"

He always woke up early, prepared thoroughly for matches, and never missed practice sessions... he showed the kind of self-discipline I didn't think someone of his age could ever show.

— Vikas Kohli, Virat's brother

A PODGY LITTLE BOY, JUST NINE YEARS OLD, trudged into the newly opened West Delhi Cricket Academy at his father's insistence.

He was one among thousands of boys who were part of the burgeoning cricket academy culture in the capital. This academy culture was far different from what it used to be just a few decades before, when you could actually count the number of good Indian cricket academies on your fingertips.

It was natural that Coach Rajkumar Sharma accept the boy as he would any new ward. He promised the father that he would take care of the budding cricketer. But it did not take long for Sharma to realize that this boy was born to play cricket and his talent demanded that he be given due care and attention. The power and timing of the little boy's strokes impressed Sharma and he was sure that within six months he would be mentoring and pushing this child to achieve his potential.

It would be just a matter of time before the name Virat Kohli would be known far and wide.

Born on November 5, 1988, to Prem and Saroj Kohli, Virat grew up in Delhi, in the Shankar Garden area. He studied in low profile schools like Vishal Bharti and Savier Convent while attending the West Delhi Cricket Academy at St. Sophia School, in Paschim Vihar.

His older siblings, Vikas and sister Bhavna,

constantly encouraged Virat to be better at his game, as did his loving parents, but when it came to cricket and any emotional decisions connected to the game, it was to Sharma that Virat went to for advice.

Virat also liked playing tennis, but his hero in sports had to be a cricketer and who better in the '90s than Sachin Tendulkar? Sharing the pitch with Tendulkar had been Virat's fantasy and he admitted later that it was rather unbelievable, even disconcerting, to share space with the great Sachin Tendulkar, because young Virat did not know how to behave in his hero's presence!

In his cricket academy that prospered in an area of west Delhi known for a hearty business culture rather than sports, Kohli stood out from the dozens of boys there. Even today, if one were to ask a Delhi resident about that part of western Delhi, they would instantly associate it not with enthusiastic sportsmen, but with speeding bikes and cars that play loud music as they zoom past.

But Virat was determined to chart a different path. He not only showed early promise of great talent, but also a focus that was unusual for someone of his age.

'Virat was chubby and naughty, but very keen to play and stood out because of his energy,' remembers

He was different because he could play long innings even when he was ▶
very young.

Sharma. 'He was different because he could play long innings even when he was very young, just nine or ten years old. He was very powerful, he could throw the ball from the boundary.'

Sharma was forthright as he explained to Virat's father Prem Kohli, that while Virat was promising, his older brother Vikas, who was also training with Sharma, did not possess an extraordinary talent.

Sharma was honest because he could make out that Prem Kohli was not like the other parents who wanted to put their children into cricket academies so that it shaved off some TV time, rather than hope that they make it big in the game.

VIRAT HAS TWO SIBLINGS: BHAVNA IS THE ELDEST AND HIS BROTHER VIKAS IS SEVEN YEARS OLDER THAN HIM.

'I leave it to you. You are like his father now and have to take care of him. Whatever you do will be best for him,' Sharma remembers Prem Kohli saying. The coach cannot forget the hope that sparkled in the father's eyes.

'He was an easy-going and nice person. He always wanted Virat to play for the country, but unfortunately he died before he could see his son play for India.'

Prem Kohli was a lawyer by education, a businessman by profession, and Virat's greatest inspiration. He was always proud of his son's early achievements, but did not live to see his son lead India to the Under-19 World Cup victory, or be part of the 2011 World Cup victory.

Virat's brother Vikas, older to him by seven years, remembers that there was no undue pressure on Virat. He was generally considered the "kid brother" since sister Bhavna was the eldest, almost nine years older than Virat.

'Coach Rajkumar Sharma did tell us early on that he found Virat immensely talented,' says Vikas. 'Virat too was ambitious, but at that age everyone dreams of playing for the country and we did not expect too much till he started playing junior state level cricket.'

Vikas says the family was confident Virat would play at least for the Ranji Trophy.

'We knew it was not easy to play international cricket. There are millions of players out there and you are just one of them. You can't take such things for granted.'

Vikas knew that his younger brother needed to be taken to various cricket grounds for matches since he had been playing in the local DDCA league at the young age of 14, and it was also important that he play in other local tournaments.

'He was too young to go to many places on his own. We had to make sure that he got there, and moreover, I was interested in watching him play. I used to drive him to the matches in and around Delhi before he was selected for proper age-group cricket,' says Vikas.

Vikas says Virat was passionate about cricket from early on and his dedication could be seen from the first day at the academy.

'He always woke up early, prepared thoroughly for matches, and never missed practice sessions. At times, our mother used to tell him to skip a practice session or two, but he showed the kind of self-discipline I didn't think someone of his age could ever show,' he adds.

Seeing Kohli on the prowl on the field or while batting during his international career, one could presume that he had always been an out-and-out natural cricketer, especially when it came to fielding. But this was not so and Coach Sharma believes it was Kohli's dedication and hard work, more than flair, that ensured he improved with each season.

'Kohli worked really hard on his fielding as he understood its importance early on. He was always willing to come in early for practice and slog out more than others, even at a young age,' remembers Sharma.

Kohli also realized that he had to control his diet and thus the chicken and mutton dishes his mom prepared lovingly, had to be limited. Curbing his diet became the norm through life for Kohli even as he developed a particular liking for Chinese and Japanese cuisine in his later years.

'In fact, when he was with me the other day on a stopover in Delhi during the home series against Australia (2013), he refused to eat the red meat offered to him. He joked that he would have to work harder in the gym if he indulged in such eating,' say.

Kohli himself remembers legendary spinner Bi. Singh Bedi's advice on fitness when he was in a junior camp and always stuck to his regimen from then on.

'I was part of an Under-15 camp which was run simultaneously with the Ranji Trophy camp,' Kohli was to say years later during an event in his academy. 'Then (Ranji Trophy) Coach Bishan sir told me to emphasize fitness and I now know how important it is to be in top fitness in cricket.'

Kohli, who was seen as the captain-in-waiting during Mahendra Singh Dhoni's reign, also showed signs of being a good captain when he was a young boy.

'He used to lead our academy sides with confidence and had the killer instinct needed to win games for the team. Confidence was not a problem with him, in fact, he was over-confident at times. For example, if the team needed wickets desperately, he would start bowling "seam-up" himself, while neglecting the main bowlers of the side. Things like that needed to be curbed, but he was always a good listener and willing learner,' remembers Sharma.

2

CHAPTER

HEAD ON!

He has transformed as a batsman over the years and is now an accomplished batsman in all forms of cricket.

— Shane Warne

KOHLI HAS ALWAYS BEEN SHARP IN THE FIELD as well as in the mind. This has helped him transcend with ease from playing junior cricket to senior cricket, from being an accomplished batsman on the domestic circuit to one who has found his bearings in the international arena.

He has been a fast learner and is willing to go that extra mile in the nets or while fielding. He made his mark in junior cricket very quickly and a string of three-figure marks for the Delhi Under-17 team, including two double centuries, saw him break into the India Under-19 side by the time he was 18.

Coach Sharma remembers how determined Kohli was, despite once being snubbed by Delhi selectors.

'He was brilliant in Under-14 matches, but unfortunately was not picked for the Delhi team. He was inconsolable at being ignored and I had to spend a lot of time to make him come to terms with the situation. I told him that if he was good, he could not be denied the chance to play good cricket. I told him not to worry about things that were not in his control. He started working even harder and promised me that he would show the selectors how good he could be,' the coach remembers.

Sharma, who was the Delhi Under-19 coach then, started giving more time to Kohli whose confidence was growing with each passing day. Sharma could make out that the little boy was maturing fast. The fat was melting away and his hunger for runs was growing.

Sharma was impressed by Kohli's ability to bat for long periods, and his immense concentration and propensity to work on weaknesses and faults in his batting. The repertoire of strokes primed and polished, he was coming out at the top in age-group cricket.

'He was definitely among the best even then. He soon bagged a double hundred in Under-15 cricket and two more at the Under-17 level playing for Delhi. He had the knack of scoring big and I have always maintained that he is a better Test player even though he excelled in One-Dayers early on in international cricket. With his technique, he is better suited for Test cricket and he will always be willing to work hard to iron out deficiencies,' adds the coach who was a Delhi Ranji and India Under-19 off-spinner.

Kohli also played for Madras Club in the Delhi and District Cricket Association league, as the West Delhi Cricket Academy did not have a team in the competitive tournament. He was a member of the Delhi Under-16 team that won the 2003-04 Vijay Merchant Trophy by defeating Mumbai in the final at Kolkata. Pace bowlers Ishant Sharma and Pradeep Sangwan were among the other prominent members of that side.

However, it was in the following year that Kohli made waves at the junior level with his two double-centuries in Under-17 cricket, but only after Coach Ajit

Kohli led the Indian Colts to victory at the ICC Under-19 World Cup ▶ at Kuala Lumpur in 2008.

Chaudhary disciplined him with warnings and posing challenges.

In the league match against Punjab in Patiala, Kohli slept at the ground after batting while the practice session was still on, which annoyed Chaudhary.

'Though he was our best batsman, I told him that he had not become such a big player that he could do what he wanted. I said he would be the twelfth man. He was apologetic and pleaded with me. Coach Sharma also spoke to me and told me to take care of the boy because he was naughty and immature, but a very good batsman. I told him, I would be playing him, but he needed the dressing down that I'd just given him,' reveals Chaudhary with a chuckle. Kohli went on to score 216 in that match, much to Chaudhary's delight.

HIGHLIGHT

THE ROYAL CHALLENGERS BANGALORE SIGNED KOHLI ON FOR $30,000, AHEAD OF THE IPL INAUGURAL SEASON IN 2008.

However, the coach had to step in once more when Kohli arrived sporting huge tattoos before the semifinal against Baroda at Eden Gardens, in Kolkata. The coach felt the boy was more concerned about style than his batting.

'He said several top players have tattoos. I told him that if such things did not affect his batting, I'd like him to score a century in the match. Kohli took up the challenge and promptly produced a knock of 250 not out,' remembers Chaudhary.

Kohli had already made it to the Delhi Ranji Trophy team by the time he was 18, and that helped him grow as a batsman while playing for the national Under-19 side. He took what he learned from one to the other – if he dominated the opposition in junior cricket because he was used to playing at a higher level, he was willing to take on the responsibility in senior cricket owing to his bigger role in junior teams.

Kohli's cocky personality stood out as did his positive attitude and vast repertoire of strokes. His fluent drives and nimble feet were a joy to watch at whichever level he played. Runs resulted in confidence and confidence in runs, when Kohli got into a superb rhythm and fed off his own successes.

Kohli was already famous for being the batsman who completed a match-saving knock in Ranji Trophy on the day of his father's death (more about which we'll read later in this book). That innings of 90 against Karnataka in 2006, heralded a grave transformation for the young cricketer, who was set to justify his name 'Virat', which means huge.

That inning brought out the youngster's pugnacious character and instantly slotted him among the men. Here was a boy who could do what was needed of him, who did not worry about circumstances on the field or off it. What more could one ask of a player?

Though his name was already being discussed on

the domestic circuit largely because of that great knock despite tragic circumstances, Kohli's immense potential caught the eye of the entire nation when he led the Indian colts to victory at the ICC Under-19 World Cup at Kuala Lumpur in 2008, and got a quick look-in for the national side.

The sprightly Kohli showed no inhibitions as he celebrated his team's triumph and gave the impression that he was prepared for and always knew he belonged at the top level. He ran about the field pumping his fists and clinching a black stump as souvenir after India completed a nerve-wracking, if lucky, 12-run win over South Africa in a rain-hit final at the Kinrara Academy Oval.

Images of Kohli screaming in delight as he lifted the trophy were beamed across the country as India witnessed the rise of another cricket star. Known then as an aggressive batsman, more than the well-rounded one that he was to emerge as in later years, Kohli helmed the team astutely as India held on for victory despite being dismissed for a measly 159 in 45.4 overs.

A two-hour break due to inclement weather saw South Africa's target being revised to 116 in 25 overs. A nagging line and length from seam bowler Ajitesh Argal, who took 2-7 in five overs with the new ball, was the highlight of India's defence of a mediocre total even as Ravindra Jadeja chipped in with two useful wickets.

But the man under the limelight was the batsman,

bowler and captain, Kohli, who also showed his ability to break partnerships whenever he came on to bowl his medium-pacers during the tournament. The energetic boy with spiked and gelled hair was suddenly the rising hero, courtesy live coverage of the final.

Kohli accumulated 235 runs in six innings including a flamboyant 100 off 74 balls against the West Indies in a league game. He had smashed the latter 50 runs in that innings off only 24 deliveries, in what was seen as one of the most delightful performances of the tournament.

The Indian colts were left celebrating the sweet victory amid a surge of fans on the ground and more rain. Kohli, who scored 19 runs in the final, remembered his late father. 'He always wanted me to do something big for India and I'm sure this would have made him proud. It was a great effort by our team. We did not put up a big total, but knew it would not be easy for South Africa to chase under lights,' Kohli said after the victory, not forgetting to thank celebrated Aussie Coach, Dav Whatmore for guiding his team.

Though Uttar Pradesh player Tanmay Srivastava scored more runs than him in the tournament (262) and also contributed a valuable 46 in the final, Kohli unquestionably was the better package during the tournament. His leadership abilities were a pleasant surprise for those following his career graph.

Vikas Kohli remembers watching the match with the family. 'It was a nice feeling. For us, at that time, playing Under-19 for India was as good as playing for the country at the senior level. We watched the match together as we usually do, at home. We have never watched matches with other people around, and as a matter of fact, I don't even go to stadiums to watch the match,' states Vikas.

Former Delhi selector, Hari Gidwani, remembers noticing the hallmarks of a captain in Kohli's performance during the Under-19 World Cup triumph and he kept that in mind.

'I did not see him much in junior cricket before the World Cup, but his performance and the way he led the side certainly caught my eye,' remembers the former Delhi and Bihar batsman. 'I thought he'd got overexcited at times and wondered how a young cricketer could get so excited. I always thought he would mellow down over time and that is why when we were looking for a new captain a few years later in the 2009-10 season, I shared my thoughts with (fellow selector) Chetan Chauhan.'

Gidwani says Kohli's approach to both batting and fielding gave him a lot of confidence. 'I saw him as a very promising athlete, a brilliant fielder. I believe that a brilliant fielder will always have the killer instinct. So I thought very positively about him and only hoped he would keep his temper in check,' adds Gidwani, who was considered by many as India-material during his heyday in the 1970s and '80s.

Kohli's performance in junior cricket led to him being one among the Under-19 players chosen under a draft system for the Indian Premier League, which was then the new big thing in cricket. The Royal Challengers Bangalore signed him up for $30,000 ahead of the inaugural season in 2008. He was now suddenly rubbing shoulders with Indian legends like Rahul Dravid and Anil Kumble, among others.

Kohli did not have an impressive first IPL season as he could manage only 165 runs in 13 innings. He was yet to break out of the mould of a brash teenager, one who did not seem to realize what life meant in top-flight cricket, despite his tremendous junior and first-class performances.

Australian spin wizard, Shane Warne, remembers telling his bowlers to test Kohli with short-pitched stuff during the first IPL season when he led the low-profile Rajasthan Royals to a surprising and dramatic victory.

'I told my bowlers to have a go at him then because we saw an opportunity there. But he has transformed as a batsman over the years and is now an accomplished batsman in all forms of cricket,' Warne said while commentating during the 2013 India-Australia series, in Chennai.

However, there was good news for Kohli as he earned a surprise call up to the national One-Day squad for the Idea Cup in Sri Lanka. He was also selected for the Champions Trophy in South Africa ahead of Robin

Uthappa and Yusuf Pathan, both members of the squad that won the 2007 Twenty20 World Cup.

Kohli, who was the second highest run-getter for India in the Emerging Players tournament in Australia in the interim, seemed to be the man selectors picked each time someone was injured.

Tendulkar and Sehwag had not been available for the Sri Lanka series, and Yuvraj Singh was injured ahead of the Champions Trophy. Kohli opened in Sri Lanka with limited success, but was now being seen as the player for the future with his willingness to take on any opportunity as a challenge.

3

CHAPTER

THE PATIENT REBEL STRIKES

I've learnt to be patient and that seems to be paying off.

– Virat Kohli

KOHLI FACED TOUGH COMPETITION FOR a slot in the middle order with Rohit Sharma and Manoj Tiwary, who were already on the selectors' radars. In fact, Kohli was more a fringe player as Rohit had already been part of the 2007 T20 World Cup team and Tiwary a proven soldier on the domestic circuit, though he had been set back by injuries.

But the selectors had already spotted Kohli's variety of strokes and a kind of aggression that was now a pre-requisite for international cricket. This meant that Kohli got chances at regular intervals. He was picked for India when still not out of his teens and being part of the team. He learnt from the best players up close and was privy to game plans being made in the dressing room, which helped him prepare for bigger challenges.

The unavailability of Sehwag and Tendulkar had thrown open the gates for Kohli's entry into the squad, but it was his willingness to bat at the top of the order in the absence of India's best opening pair that really got him the first feel of international cricket when still three months shy of his 20th birthday.

It was August 18, 2008. Kohli opened with senior Delhi pro Gautam Gambhir, only to see his state-mate clean bowled off the second delivery of the innings by a trademark Chaminda Vaas delivery that moved just enough to beat the bat.

Kohli plodded on for a while, content playing dot balls and singles early on. It was proving to be a testing baptism as India inched forward to a slow 23 in almost eight overs with Gambhir already back in the pavilion. Kohli too was out a little later as he tried a drive, but was trapped lbw by seam bowler Nuwan Kulasekara.

India was bowled out for a meager 146 and went down by eight wickets. With Gambhir now unavailable for the second game, Kohli went in with makeshift opener Irfan Pathan and contributed a crucial 67-ball 37 in the low scoring game that helped level the series.

After pace bowler Zaheer Khan had sliced through the Sri Lankan top order with 4-21 including the big wickets of Kumar Sangakkara and Mahela Jayawardene, Kohli came on to keep the run chase on track. Kohli took his time settling in and then executed some fine shots on the off side as well as a few streaky ones behind the wicket to put India on the way to its target of 143.

Kohli was out playing a loose drive, the chase wobbled and seven wickets were lost to indiscretion. It was left to Captain Dhoni to top-score with 39 and figure in a crucial stand with Subramaniam Badrinath (27 not out).

It was ironical that the manner of the unimpressive win was attributed to the lack of specialist openers when Kohli was the second highest run-getter for India

In his 14th One-Day game, Kohli played all around the wicket and ▶ showed patience and initiative.

at the top of the order. Even Captain Dhoni did not mention Kohli's contribution during the prize distribution ceremony as he credited Zaheer for the victory and also praised Chennai Super Kings team-mate Badrinath (27 not out) with whom Dhoni added 60 for the sixth wicket.

HIGHLIGHT

KOHLI GOT HIS FIRST THREE-FIGURE MARK AGAINST SRI LANKA IN HIS 14TH ONE-DAY GAME (107 OFF 114 BALLS).

Kohli looked more confident in the remaining matches of the series, which India won 3-2. He smashed a fluent 25 before being dismissed to a direct throw run out in the third game and then produced knocks of 54 and 31 in the last two.

Though not yet established, Kohli had shown in the chances he got that he was definitely not out of depth at the top level. Probably even Dhoni realized that he had found one of the men he would need in the coming years when the likes of Dravid and Laxman would not be around in Test cricket.

In a bid to encourage the young Delhi batsman, he asked him to come on the stage to receive the trophy. Kohli had thus wrapped his hands around a trophy at the senior level too. He was destined to add the senior World Cup victory to the junior World Cup already won, but for the time being, this was good enough.

However, Kohli had to wait for more than a year to make his next ODI appearance in September 2009. He got to face only two deliveries for his two not out in the low-profile Compaq Cup final in Sri Lanka as Sachin Tendulkar knocked up 138 to help India score 319-5 and win by 46 runs.

He got to play a string of games during the Champions Trophy in South Africa as Yuvraj was not around. A couple of insignificant games later, he got his first Man of the Match award in a league game against a weak West Indies side. Kohli struck an unbeaten 79 off 104 balls with nine fours and two sixes as India reached an unchallenging target of 130 at the Wanderers in Johannesburg with seven wickets remaining, but still failed to go beyond the league stage.

Kohli, who had by now made a habit of playing some dot balls early on in a bid to get set, conceded that it was what he always had in mind.

'I've been hitting the ball well for the past few months and was confident going in to bat today,' Kohli said at the awards ceremony. 'I've learnt to be patient and that seems to be paying off.'

It was clear by now that Kohli knew the scheme of things. He was a regular part of One-Day sides though not always getting to play, let alone a regular batting slot. He moved up and down the order especially when the top three in the order – Tendulkar, Sehwag, and Gambhir were around.

Some more games at home gave Kohli breathing

space as India faced familiar foes Sri Lanka and competitive adversaries Australia. Kohli chipped in with some useful runs here and there, but the big innings was still to come.

Kohli got his first three-figure mark against Sri Lanka in his 14th One-Day game as he took the game away from the visiting side in the company of Gambhir. It was a fluent knock from Kohli in which he played all around the wicket and showed enough of both patience and initiative.

India overhauled Sri Lanka's huge total of 315 with ease as Kohli struck 107 off 114 balls with 11 fours and a six, once taking four consecutive fours off pace bowler Lasith Malinga, whose round arm action was disconcerting for batsmen, as were his lethal deliveries. He was not the easiest to get runs off, as one had seen both in international cricket and the IPL, but Kohli annihilated his bowling in what was an important phase of the game.

Gambhir eventually outscored him with 150, but Kohli had done his job in style and got the opportunity to punch the air and jump in the fashion that was to become his trademark in later years. Though Kohli took his time settling into the side as he did with each of his innings, it has to be remembered that India was playing some of its best cricket during this time and the teams – both during Tests and limited overs – were more or less settled.

In that span of a few years, India reached the

number 1 ranking in Test cricket and lifted the World Cup as well. At times like these, opportunities often take their time coming. Kohli made the most of the chances, determined to carve out his destiny and build on his fledgling international career.

Though the first century took some time coming, there were to be several more in the next couple of years, as Kohli established himself in the One-Day side and others began relying on the plucky batsman.

He got some good knocks in One-Dayers in the Indian sub-continent while also figuring in Twenty20 teams for India after showing his worth in the IPL over the years. He notched up another century against Sri Lanka during a tri-series in Bangladesh and also got tons against Australia and New Zealand at home in 2010.

India seemed to have several options for building its team for the 2011 World Cup, while it carried the heavy tag of 'favourites'. The Dhoni-led side had been developing well in both batting and bowling under the astute supervision of Coach Gary Kirsten. Would Kohli be an integral part of the side? Would he get to play in the big games?

That was a question in the minds of selectors, players and fans during a time when every discussion seemed to find its way to the World Cup. It did not get any bigger for cricket, because it was being played on the sub-continent and that too when the Indian team was doing well.

Though the familiarity of conditions would have given the selectors and team management the confidence to pick the gutsy lad, Kohli settled the issue with a score of 54 and 87 against South Africa at Durban and Port Elizabeth just a month ahead of the World Cup. Kohli was warming up well and his hunger for runs looked insatiable.

Would he be one of the heroes for India if they were to win the World Cup?

4

CHAPTER

THE GENTLEMAN'S GAME

Sachin Tendulkar has carried the burden of the nation for 21 years. It's time we carried him on our shoulders.

— Virat Kohli

THE FESTIVE ATMOSPHERE OUTSIDE THE Sher-e-Bangla Stadium in Mirpur on the eve of the 2011 World Cup opener had to be seen to be believed. Thousands of fans clambered on to trucks and tempos, cars and motorbikes. Their faces were painted in national colours, they cheered for the teams and waved Bangladesh flags.

It was like a celebration in advance that beat even the annual March 26 Independence Day festivities. Bangladesh was hosting the World Cup for the first time, and fans were hoping for an encore of the 2007 World Cup in the Caribbean when India had been heaved out by its lightweight neighbour in the early stages.

It was being seen as a grudge match, a chance for India to avenge the defeat four years ago and for Shakib-al-Hasan's men to bruise the ego of the former champions once more.

But in what was an anti-climactic start for the home side, Sehwag set the tone with a punched four through the covers off Shafiqul Islam that stunned the crowd into silence. It was only the first of many such hits off his bat that day. The big-hitting opener was on way to a stroke-filled 175, which was the performance of the match.

Sehwag had always been one for the big stage, but what was reassuring for Indian fans was Kohli's smashing century in his World Cup debut. Carrying on in splendid form from South Africa, Kohli produced a solid knock to reach the ton off the penultimate delivery of the match.

It had not been an easy decision for Dhoni to leave out Suresh Raina for Kohli, but the 100-not-out batsman from Delhi had sealed his place in the side. Kohli, batting at number 4, smashed eight fours and two sixes off only 83 deliveries as India reached 370-4 and eventually won by 87 runs. Kohli exhibited a variety of strokes, but his flowing drives were a standout feature.

Kohli did not get a fixed position to bat at and was shuffled from number three to seven during the tournament, even as Yuvraj Singh hit terrific form and was used judiciously by Dhoni. Kohli's next best was 59 batting at number 3 against the West Indies, a game won easily by India at Chennai.

In the final, Kohli produced a useful knock of 35 and figured in an important 83-run stand for the fourth wicket with Gambhir, who top scored with 97. It was a stand in which the strike was rotated sensibly, a point noted by Dhoni after the game.

Though he was not one to look out for in a star-studded lineup, his growing maturity was being noticed. If Kohli played according to the needs of the team, he was also articulate whenever he spoke to the media. It was probably the first time people thought of him as a

Kohli was in prime form in 2012, scoring 364 runs in 16 matches with ▶ two half-centuries and was named captain for the 2013 season.

future captain because till then he had not even been a certainty in limited overs sides, leave alone Tests.

Though a number of Indian players spoke about the Indian team and how they had aimed to win the World Cup for Tendulkar, Kohli stole the hearts of millions with his judicious selection of words. His ode to Tendulkar, who was carried on the shoulders by jubilant team-members after the victory at the Wankhede Stadium in Mumbai, expressed the feelings of players, fans, and experts alike and his heartfelt speech will be remembered for long.

HIGHLIGHT

IN THE FOURTH SEASON, KOHLI WAS THE ONLY PLAYER RETAINED BY THE ROYAL CHALLENGERS BANGALORE AHEAD OF FRESH AUCTIONS.

'Sachin Tendulkar has carried the burden of the nation for 21 years. It's time we carried him on our shoulders,' Kohli said of his idol, who had made his international debut when Kohli was only a one-year-old.

Kohli consistently produced big knocks in One-Dayers, but he was still not a serious contender in the Test side at best a contestant for the number six slot and looked out of depth when given a chance during a tour of the West Indies in 2011, where he debuted along with Abhinav Mukund and Praveen Kumar at Kingston, Jamaica.

He had knocks of 84 and 91 during a five-game

One-Day series in the run-up to the Tests, but could only manage 76 in three games of the longest format. India, playing without Tendulkar, who had opted out, understandably looked jaded because of the World Cup and IPL that had just preceded the June-July tour and could only prevail 1-0.

It was one of those few times in life that Kohli had not utilized opportunities. The mediocre opposition and friendly surfaces offered a good chance for him to produce some notable knocks, but probably the laggard attitude of the team, which had refused to push for victory on that tour, rubbed on to him.

Kohli did somewhat better when the West Indies toured India in November that year. It was again a low-profile team led by Darren Sammy, but a gritty one that ran India closer than the 2-0 scoreline would suggest.

Kohli made 52 and 63 in the Mumbai Test, which ended in a thrilling draw with scores level in the two innings and India having lost nine wickets in the last innings, to be in contention for a Test berth. In the months to come, Yuvraj Singh went on to fight cancer and Suresh Raina was repeatedly found wanting in terms of technique, giving Kohli a little breathing space.

In the meanwhile, he did not get to play on the tour of England where India was whitewashed 4-0, but was again the main contender for the last specialist batsman's slot on the tour of Australia as India's performance in Tests plummeted. Experienced players like Dravid, Tendulkar, and Laxman were under fire as India went on to lose eight Tests on the trot in away games starting with the tour of England.

It was one of the more testing tours for India in December-January (2011-12). The Indian team had won the World Cup at the beginning of the year, but then lost 4-0 to England in a Test series. It was hard to say whether the team was going up or down; whether it was a matter of Tests or One-Dayers or playing at home and abroad.

For Kohli, it was a do-or-die chance and he was not coming out with flying colours yet. Four successive failures during the Tests at Melbourne and Sydney with a highest score of 23 and an aggregate of 44 runs meant Kohli was running out of chances.

With his performances, he could not be assured of a place in the next two Tests in Sydney and Adelaide and the team-management had to take a call on whether to give him a longer run or not. Kohli was anxious as he needed just one good knock to maintain his place in the side because of the other failures.

Kohli's coach Rajkumar Sharma recollects that Kohli was quite apprehensive midway into the series.

'I've never ever seen him nervous or down, even when his father was ill or passed away. But in Australia, getting out early in four innings, he was not sounding confident at all. I'd even told his brother Vikas that I'd fly down to Australia to encourage him,' remembers Sharma.

But Kohli gained confidence after knocks of 44 and 75 at Perth and a big one was to follow in Adelaide that helped him establish himself in the Test team.

'I told him not to worry and just try to perform if he got a chance in the third Test. I feel it was very nice of Dhoni to show faith in him and he was confident after the 40-odd he got in the first innings at Perth. He said: "Don't worry sir, I'll get runs." Then we started talking positive things about his batting and discussed the fact that the whole team was not doing well, not just him. Then, after the 70-odd in the second innings, his mindset changed completely. Finally, the Adelaide century changed his career,' says Sharma.

Though Ricky Ponting and Captain Michael Clarke slammed double-centuries, Kohli gave a glimmer of hope to the Indian side for the long run. In the immediate context, his innings was at best a face-saving one, but it was one that boosted his own confidence and that of the selectors in him.

Kohli smashed 116 that hot January in Adelaide after some early probing deliveries from Peter Siddle. The boundaries were not easy coming in the first part of his innings, when he was content with singles and twos. He got to probably the most important century of his career with a push to the off side for two and indulged in a somewhat restrained celebration, by his standards, considering the enormity of the feat he had just achieved.

Kohli, who had survived being almost run out in the

preceding delivery in a hurry to get to his hundred, kissed his helmet and appreciated the applause. His 237-ball knock contained 11 fours and a six and was the biggest redeeming feature of an Indian team that was otherwise down in the dumps.

He then produced a whirlwind 86-ball 133 with 16 fours and two sixes in a CB Series match against Sri Lanka at Hobart. This knock was selected as the top ODI batting performance for 2012, at the ESPN Cricinfo Awards.

The One-Day knocks came regularly, but the Adelaide Test century had been a turning point in his career. Another of Kohli's top knocks was round the corner and came about a year after the World Cup game at the same Mirpur stadium where he had notched up an unbeaten 100.

Kohli produced a career-best 183 off 148 balls with 22 fours and a six to help reach a huge target of 330 set by Pakistan in an Asia Cup match in March 2012, that too with 13 deliveries to spare.

It was an innings that Pakistan captain Misbah-ul-Haq called the 'best innings I have ever seen'.

Now not just a regular in the Test team, but one of the mainstays along with Cheteshwar Pujara, Kohli was again among runs as Michael Clark led a low-profile squad on a tour of India in February-March 2013. Though the team was recognized as a weak one, the four Tests preceding dismal performances.

Kohli scored a valuable 107, batting at number five in the first innings of the opening Test at Chennai, featuring in an important 128-run fifth-wicket stand with double-centurion Dhoni as India wrested the initiative on a plank provided by Tendulkar's 81.

Australia had made a decent beginning with 380, but India scored a massive 572 to gain momentum in the series even as the visiting side put up its worst performance ever on the Indian soil, losing 0-4. It was payback time as India had exacted revenge for a similar series score on the tour of Australia, just over a year before.

Though others like Cheteshwar Pujara, Shikhar Dhawan, Ravichandran Ashwin and Ravindra Jadeja were the main architects of the victory, Kohli batted consistently at Hyderabad (34), Mohali (67 not out and 34), and Delhi (1 and 41) to remain an important part of the team.

While Kohli proved himself to be one for the big stage during the World Cup and as one worthy of taking over from big names in the Test lineup, he had already established himself as the kind of showman that a team needed for the IPL.

Kohli had an average first two seasons in the IPL (2008 and 2009) but scored 307 runs in 13 innings in the fourth season and was the only player retained by the Royal Challengers Bangalore ahead of fresh auctions.

He then played a big role in Bangalore reaching the

final of the 2011 edition, held immediately after the World Cup, with Chris Gayle regaling the crowds at the top of the order. Kohli accumulated 557 runs and Gayle 608.

Kohli was in prime form in 2012, scoring 364 runs in 16 matches with two half-centuries and was named captain for the 2013 season.

CHAPTER 5

GROWING WITH CAUTION

I feel blessed when people compare me with Sachin, but I keep myself focused on my performance and not on such comparisons. I literally worship him, so I don't read too much into the comparison.

— Virat Kohli

THIS MAY PROBABLY NOT GO WITH HIS PERSONALITY, but Kohli is actually pretty conservative with his batting. He generally likes to bat himself in and plays straight early on. He gets the bulk of his runs with drives through the off side and with the whips through mid-wicket before he gets on with his pulls and square drives.

He would much rather depend on conventional shots and has consciously tried to cut out the riskier ones from his repertoire. That is why you'll see him play the difficult back-foot drive through covers more than the square cut, the inside-out hit over covers rather than the reverse-sweep.

Kohli has his game clearly worked out in his mind with the firm knowledge of the probability of success against every kind of bowling. He is always open to discussing technique with coaches and does not have an inflated ego. Apart from his God-given talent and hunger for success, he has developed a keen eye for the game, adaptability and the aptitude to soak in what is best for him.

So, it is normal for him to talk to the coach of whichever team he is playing for, as it is for him to call up Coach Rajkumar Sharma on an almost daily basis.

'We talk about technique practically every single day,' says Coach Sharma. 'At the academy, he comes an hour before practice time when there is not much of a rush and I tell him what to do. He has discussed his technique with (national coaches) Gary Kirsten and Duncan Fletcher at length and came back to me to discuss what he learnt from them.'

Sharma says Kohli makes sure he understands what he has been told and then puts into practice what he feels needs to be modified or corrected.

'I have told him that whosoever tries to tell him anything is his well-wisher and wants him to do well. However, he can't follow everything and needs to implement only those things which suit him, otherwise he'll be confused. There will always be people telling him to hold the bat in a slightly different way or work on his back-lift, or something similar. All those things can't be introduced in his batting and that's why he takes my word. He talks to everyone, but the final decision on what and how to inculcate something in his batting is arrived at together after discussing it at length,' says Sharma.

Former Delhi selector Hari Gidwani too, has observed that Kohli has worked hard on his batting through the years. Having watched him play for Delhi, Gidwani remembers him as a focused batsman who always realized his mistakes very quickly. He even draws comparisons with Tendulkar.

'Have a look at Sachin and Virat and you'll see the back-lift is very straight unlike many others whose bat may come from the slip and gully region,' says Gidwani. 'The beauty of Virat is that he plays the ball

Kohli gets the bulk of his runs from drives through the off side. ▶

with ease, has a lot of time to play his shots, which are silken rather than played with brute force.'

Gidwani picks Kohli's shot through the covers from within the crease as the best.

'Driving the ball through the covers off the backfoot is the most difficult shot and he executes it with ease. Another shot of his which I like is the one he plays between mid-wicket and square-leg, which almost always gets him a boundary. He has several signs of a high quality player and that is something which has ensured success and will take him further in international cricket,' says Gidwani.

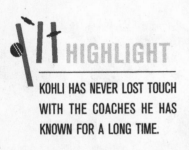

HIGHLIGHT

KOHLI HAS NEVER LOST TOUCH WITH THE COACHES HE HAS KNOWN FOR A LONG TIME.

Kohli is one player who you can expect will take on any challenge that is thrown at him, including getting through with some mid-overs in limited overs games. Though his seam bowling is yet to give confidence like Sourav Ganguly's did, at least in seaming conditions, he is always enthusiastic while bowling. It shows that he is always in the game and ready to do what the skipper wants him to.

The fact that he could establish himself in the Indian team despite competing against both seniors and contemporaries, is proof of his persistence and application. He watches other batsmen his age with fondness and has gone on record several times praising Rohit Sharma, who is his direct competition for India slots.

Kohli might have had a tough time before he made it to the India side due to personal upheavals and a self-confessed struggle to keep focus, but that probably fine-tuned him for the challenges ahead.

Having to regain single-mindedness and diligence at such a crucial period in his life, he not only charted his way to success, but found the method to do so despite trying times. That is something essential in hectic modern day cricket, when you push down.

After all, it is not just talent that keeps you at the top. You have to study the opposition, rework your plans and keep refining your game. Kohli learnt to keep distractions at bay and the learning curve of his teenage years defined him.

Rohit, the Mumbai batsman, was ahead in the pecking order when Kohli came on to the scene, but he had to give way to Kohli despite the backing he had from the selectors and team management. They were in no doubt about the technique and versatility that Rohit possessed and the support that he got was well deserved, but Rohit could not justify the persistence with him as he wasted the chances given to him. Like Kohli, he too had made it to the top level amid adulation. The lures of the IPL after the 2007 Twenty20 World Cup victory got him a much-more financially attractive IPL offer for Mumbai Indians since he had played with the India cap. He was another batsman for all formats of the game and seemed to have so much time to play his strokes. But Kohli was the one to grab his opportunities, instilling the kind of discipline needed to thrive in the face of testing bowling and situations.

The hunger that Kohli showed, soon lifted him much above the others of his generation and it was no surprise that he overtook Gambhir in the race for captaincy as he was named Dhoni's deputy for the 2012 Asia Cup.

Kohli also has the ability to perform on the big stage. Look up his career and you'll see him dazzle at the Under-19 World Cup, the World Cup, and in matches against top adversaries like Australia and Pakistan. He has an unwavering belief in his own batting and works towards attaining his goals.

'Virat has always loved challenges and wants to do well against teams like Australia and Pakistan. He is not scared of anyone – be it any opposition or any bowler. Aggression has been his strength and though he has crossed the line at times, has managed to hold on to his own and use it to his advantage,' adds Sharma.

Coach Sharma says Kohli is always involved in the team's goings-on and is not the sort of cricketer who could just take his place in the field without being bothered about how to help the team dominate.

'He has a tremendous cricketing brain and leadership qualities, even now he tries to adjust the field when Dhoni is the captain. He is a good team man and wants his team to win. He once opened the batting for Delhi in a Ranji Trophy match against Saurashtra when Delhi was facing relegation and wanted to earn a bonus point. Virat scored a quick knock (88 not out, 12 fours, two sixes) on a green-top at Roshanara Club ground to help chase the target in quick time. That is the kind of commitment he brings to the field,' Sharma points out.

The fact that he is so regularly in touch with people known to him for a long time indicates that he is firmly rooted.

Ajit Chaudhary, who was the coach of junior Delhi teams in which Kohli played, says he has not seen any change in him over the years.

'He respects me and other officials like he used to and the change in his stature has not affected the way he talks to us,' says Chaudhary. 'He says he remembers our times together during BCCI age-group tournaments and that he often shares those moments with his team members in the Indian dressing room. The other day, he introduced me to Suresh Raina and told him that I was the man he was always talking about.'

Kohli has been down-to-earth whenever he has spoken to the media and has reiterated that one should not lose focus.

'I feel blessed when people compare me with Sachin, but I keep myself focused on my performance and not on such comparisons. I literally worship him, so I don't read too much into the comparison. I keep myself

focused on my performance,' Kohli said during the
television show *Aap Ki Adaalat* on India TV in
December 2012.

6

CHAPTER

SOLEMN TRIBUTE

You could say that he did it for our father or whatever, but the fact was that he was more mature after that day.

– Vikas Kohli

IT WAS A WINTER MORNING none of the players at the Ferozeshah Kotla ground could ever forget.

News trickled in that overnight batsman Virat Kohli had lost his father in the wee hours. Prem Kohli had suffered a brain stroke. Delhi was in a precarious position, facing the embarrassing prospect of following-on against Karnataka, and Kohli's absence would be badly felt as he had been batting well for his 40 runs.

But that was if Kohli did not turn up! Kohli not only made a dramatic entry into the stadium that stunned everyone, but he also went on to make a solid 90 in the company of Puneet Bisht (156) to avoid batting again as well as avoiding a likely defeat.

The runs he made that morning showed no signs of the trauma the 18-year-old was going through. Advised by some to resume batting and by others to stay put at home, Kohli braved the death of the man who was instrumental in putting him on the path to stardom; the loss probably provided him with the extra fire he needed to go on to the next level.

As if there had not been enough drama on the day, Kohli was given out lbw when replays clearly showed his bat had brushed his pad. He trudged back to the pavilion in disappointment and viewed replays of his dismissal with distress.

'I was in Sydney with my academy team when I got a call from Virat. He burst out crying as he told me about his father's death when the match was still in progress. I asked what the position of the match was.

He told me Delhi was in dire straits and asked me what he should do,' remembers Sharma.

It was the kind of situation very few people face in life and only the rare ones actually brave it the way Kohli did. Even Sharma was caught unawares and was at his wits' end.

'I could not make up my mind and promised to call him 15 minutes later. I thought of the position of the match and his own personal situation before I called him and asked him what he'd like to do. "This is the time to show your character" is all I had to tell him and he had decided what needed to be done. "Yes sir, even I want to bat," was his reply and the issue had been settled,' he says.

But Sharma was not expecting Kohli to call him up again as he did.

'He was crying again, this time because he felt he had been unlucky to be given out on 90. He said he had just missed a century for no fault of his.'

Virat's elder brother Vikas says it was not moral support that helped Virat turn up for the match, rather it was something that was taken for granted.

'It was a difficult time for all of us and we knew it. I did not know the situation of the match, but I knew that it was his first Ranji Trophy season and he needed to play whenever he got the chance. I asked him

In the wee hours of December 16, 2006, Prem Kohli passed away. ▶

whether he wanted to go for the match and that he had to make a choice. He spoke to his coach and decided to play. It was a difficult decision, but he made the choice. You could say that he did it for our father or whatever, but the fact was that he was more mature after that day,' recalls Vikas.

HIGHLIGHT

KOHLI BRAVED THE DEATH OF THE MAN WHO WAS INSTRUMENTAL IN PUTTING HIM ON THE PATH TO STARDOM; THE LOSS PROBABLY PROVIDED HIM WITH THE EXTRA FIRE HE NEEDED TO GO ON TO THE NEXT LEVEL.

Kohli had done his job that particular day, his stature rising in the eyes of the fraternity. He went back to attend the funeral of his father late in the afternoon (around 3.30 pm).

Kohli's batting partner Bisht said it was a pretty odd situation for a youngster like him, who was himself in his first first-class season.

'Not all the players knew about his father's death before Virat walked into the dressing room. He told us about it and went about preparing to go in to bat as he usually does, but was, of course, quieter that day. The team management and players asked him to reconsider his decision to resume batting, but he was determined to play,' remembers Bisht.

The young pair, both in their first Ranji season, went about doing their jobs doggedly, but without actually planning their partnership.

'He batted normally, but we did not talk much. His batting was immaculate and he was all concentration. I appreciated his shots, encouraged him, but I did not know what else to do. I was not sure whether he needed more encouragement and whether he'd welcome more words from me,' Bisht reminisces.

Bisht knew then that this boy was different from the rest.

'I was amazed to see his dedication because I'm sure anyone else would have left the match. To keep such a tragedy out of your mind and bat on against a good opposition was one of the biggest tests of his life. After all, it was not just a relative, but his father he had just lost. It showed his strength of character and only the rare ones can do something like that,' Bisht adds.

Kohli's grit was praised not just by former and present Delhi players like Chetan Chauhan and Mithun Manhas, but also by Karnataka coach Venkatesh Prasad.

'When we heard the news, the entire team walked up to him and offered our condolences,' the former India pace bowler said at the end of the day's play. 'His innings showed what stuff he's made of. It's not easy to connect to the game and you tend to have an overflow of emotions, but he played a superb knock.'

Ajit Chaudhary, who had been the coach of the Delhi Under-17 teams that Kohli played in, remembers that Kohli gained in stature after that one deed.

'He was always the one who took up challenges, like I'd seen in junior teams. But once he came on to bat at such a difficult time and actually saved Delhi from embarrassment, everyone in the fraternity knew there was a special player around,' remembers Chaudhary.

'There was the general impression that he was a rebel, that he needed to be disciplined time and again, but from then on, we could not doubt his commitment. We all knew it was a matter of time before he would go on to play at a higher level of cricket; his talent had never been in question,' adds Chaudhary.

Kohli had already been noticed in junior cricket with several big knocks, but that day – on December 16, 2006, he had matured beyond his years and was soon to be recognized as one of the brightest cricketers in the country.

7

CHAPTER

PLAYING BY THE BOOK

Rohit Sharma, Suresh Raina and Virat Kohli are all equally talented, but Virat's fighting nature and his eagerness to make chances count works in his favour. He is mentally very strong.

— Kapil Dev,
former India captain

VIRAT KOHLI IS ONE BATSMAN ALL FORMER PLAYERS of repute have praised. They've seen a player of caliber and versatility in Kohli and consider him good captaincy material.

He has been applauded at different points in his career for his positive and determined approach to batting and fielding. He has eased himself into all three formats of the game and has ensured that he does not let go of his hold by delivering consistent performances, which is why several former captains have thrown their weight behind Kohli.

With 'Captain Cool' Dhoni too admiring the man for his temperament, he was definitely the captain in waiting by 2013, and it probably did him no harm as Dhoni continued at the helm, giving him more time to understand the gradations of the game.

Dhoni termed his understudy a 'fighting character' who 'knows how to soak pressure' and has a 'brilliant temperament' as Kohli produced several useful knocks for his captain. Be it One-Dayers or Tests, Kohli could always be depended upon and there are those who felt that Kohli should have been handed the reins when the team was not doing well under Dhoni.

Kohli was the only option for captain when India was besieged during a home series against England in 2012, as openers Virender Sehwag and Gautam Gambhir struggled to hold their places, and opening great Sunil Gavaskar, even suggested his name on the television channel NDTV as he advocated that Dhoni needed to be replaced.

'Virat Kohli might bring the flair of Tiger Pataudi in his captaincy,' Gavaskar went on to say. 'If he knows that he will be appointed for a longer term, he will show dynamism, aggression, panache, and class. Except for his mouthing abuses when he reaches a milestone, I like everything about him.'

Kohli was working on his temperament, and the abuses were not as frequent, as he worked up a comfortable lead over other contemporaries by the time Australia visited India for a four-Test series in February-March 2013.

'Rohit Sharma, Suresh Raina, and Virat Kohli are all equally talented, but Virat's fighting nature and his eagerness to make chances count works in his favour, he is mentally very strong,' World Cup winning captain Kapil Dev said about Kohli during a programme on the news channel Headlines Today.

Though his efforts in limited overs got him a huge following among the people, the gurus of the game had become sworn converts only after the Adelaide Test century.

In fact, former captain Sourav Ganguly, after seeing two useful knocks at the challenging Perth pitch, had almost predicted a big one from Kohli at Adelaide.

'At some stage he has to move up the batting order,' Ganguly said while commentating for ESPN during India's tour of Australia in 2011-12. 'I see him going up the ladder, he is a very good player, hopefully he will

▲ *Dhoni called his understudy a 'fighting character' who 'knows how to soak pressure' and has a 'brilliant temperament'.*

better his performance at Adelaide. It is going to be a good batting surface.'

By the time Australia toured India in February-March 2013, Ganguly was sure that Kohli was the man to carry India's hopes, and not only as captain.

'I think much of Indian cricket's future will rest on Virat Kohli now. I see a lot of talent in India, but they should be given time to settle down at the international level,' he said while speaking at a function in Kolkata.

Former Australian captain Ian Chappell too had seen signs of greatness in Kohli during the tour Down Under and noticed that the Delhi batsman was not easily satisfied and often egged himself on to do more.

HIGHLIGHT

IAN CHAPPELL PRAISED KOHLI'S EFFORT TO COVER HIS STUMPS AND NOT GIVE THE BOWLERS A GOOD LOOK AT THEM, HE FELT THAT IT WAS ONE WAY OF FRUSTRATING BOWLERS.

'He is aware of one of his problems as you can see him talk to himself about playing straighter instead of flicking across the line,' Chappell said. 'I think he is a smart enough cricketer, has captained under-age level so a lot of people feel he has a good cricket brain and from what I have seen, it looks like that.'

Chappell praised Kohli's effort to cover his stumps and not give the bowlers a good look at them, because he felt that it was one way of frustrating bowlers.

'What I like about him is his back foot defence and the way he covers the off stump. I like top order batsmen to cover the off stump. This is extremely important because 60-70 percent of dismissals are caught behind the wicket. If you cover your off stump, you are giving yourself the best chance not to get out that way,' Chappell said.

'My coach told me when I was a very young kid: if the bowler gets to see your stumps, he does not feel like he can hit them. If he sees them, he feels he can hit them,' Chappel said on ESPN during the coverage of India's tour of Australia.

VVS Laxman feels Kohli climbed up a few rungs with that century at Adelaide, because he was under tremendous pressure with some early failures in Test cricket.

'People wanted him out of the team. He did not do well in Melbourne and Sydney, but went in with a positive mindset at Perth and then getting a hundred in Adelaide, chased his mindset,' Laxman said on Star Sports during Australia's tour of India in 2013 when asked what he felt about Kohli as a fellow batsman.

'Getting your first Test hundred in Australia will give confidence to any player and he has been a changed batsman from then on. He is very balanced and always keen to get runs. Even when he is getting runs, he wants to work on his batting,' added Laxman.

Former Delhi batsman and selector Hari Gidwani hopes Kohli will be there for the long run.

'I find him one of the most amazing players today as he has almost all the strokes in the book,' said Gidwani with pride, because he had pushed the young lad during his Ranji Trophy days. 'I wish he keeps the form. He has the caliber to survive overseas, but should either develop a hook shot or stay out of the line of the bouncer. In those conditions, he will be tested frequently.'

CHAPTER 8

THE BEST IS YET TO COME

I know it takes time, but I think I have matured enough to start an organization for children who cannot afford an education or play any sport. If I'm able to inspire kids to achieve something, that will be my biggest achievement.

— Virat Kohli

IT IS NOT EASY TO DEVELOP AS A CRICKETER when the enthusiastic media is quick to mark you out for the future or label you as the 'next best thing in Indian cricket.' Especially so, when you've made your mark in junior international cricket and your appearance on the field on the day of your father's death is reported widely.

With the marketing world looking eagerly for new cricket stars in a country where world-class sportsmen are not produced every other day, Kohli very soon developed a persona that appealed to youngsters and he became an advertisers' delight.

Growing up at a time when the media's perspective seemed lost to overzealousness, Kohli confessed to having almost lost his mind, before ensuring his head stayed in place.

The fact that he grew up and played his cricket in Delhi, ensured that he was always in the line of vision, unlike someone like Dhoni, who grew up in the backwaters of Indian cricket.

If maturing as a player has its challenges when you hail from a small city, there are also several trials when you grow up in a big one. If Virender Sehwag and Gautam Gambhir were already firm pillars of the national side, there was also another batsman in Shikhar Dhawan who had been in the reckoning for some years.

Kohli had to make a mark for himself from among a multitude of names, the Under-19 victory proving both a catalyst and a distractor. Though he had already done his bit in senior domestic cricket, the junior World Cup conquest under his leadership catapulted him to sudden stardom.

He conceded that the time immediately after the 2008 Under-19 World Cup victory had not been easy.

'There were some distractions as we had just come to the IPL after the Under-19 World Cup win. I was suddenly playing with foreign stars and could not handle all the attention well. I realized I was on the wrong track and that I would not be able to play for India that way,' he was to tell reporters at the time.

Life outside the cricket ground was proving to be a challenge for Kohli as it was likely to be for any teenager bestowed with so much attention and Coach Sharma had to step in to help the batsman take control.

'The Under-19 World Cup had just been won and he seemed to be losing focus, and there came a period when I'd have to control him, even scold him,' reveals Sharma. 'He had just been handed an IPL contract and the sudden fame could have been difficult to digest for anyone.'

Sharma had to remind him about the basic fact that he was a cricketer and everything else came later.

'I can very well understand how it would have been

The spiked-gelled hairstyle, stubble and tattoos were a hit and his ▶
aggression a major selling point.

for him considering that he was only 18 years old and suddenly he was getting so much media attention and money. When you see crowds following you, trying to talk to you, one is bound to feel big. I had to take care of him at the time, tell him that everything he was getting was because of cricket. He soon realized that he could not ignore cricket for anything else. He promised that he would not deviate from doing what he was best at,' says Sharma.

HIGHLIGHT

BY 2012, KOHLI HAD ACCRUED 1,733 RUNS IN 31 ONE-DAY INTERNATIONALS AT A SUPERB AVERAGE OF 66.65 THAT INCLUDED EIGHT CENTURIES AND SIX HALF-CENTURIES.

'When he was selected for India the first time, he said, "Don't worry sir, I'll make it big now and play for a long time for the country." I knew he had that kind of aptitude and attention and was assured he would do what he had decided,' he adds.

Though determined and doughty on the field, Kohli is known as a jovial character off it and one who can regale teammates and lighten the atmosphere in the dressing room.

People who interacted with him even during the tumultuous period which saw him lose his father but gain cricketing stature, remember that though not the most innovative batsmen on the field, he was not averse to trying out new styles off it.

In fact, he once tried a hairstyle that earned him the nick name 'Chiku'.

'He came into the team dressing room with his hair gelled up in what I though was a weird way. He asked me how he was looking and I said he reminded me of a popular Hindi cartoon character called 'Chiku'. Other Delhi players started calling him by that name and that name has stuck to him and even the India players call him by that name,' says his Delhi junior coach Ajit Chaudhary.

Both the hairstyle and nickname stuck with Kohli for years to come.

As Kohli broke into international cricket and became the fastest Indian to bag 1,000 and then 3,000 runs in One-Day internationals, there were the inevitable comparisons to Sachin Tendulkar, which he promptly and maturely declined as heart-warming, but improper.

Kohli's aggression, which he conceded as having carried since his early days in cricket when he broke several bats in fits of fury, was to settle down rather well and he was named the vice-captain of the One-Day side for the 2012 Asia Cup in Bangladesh.

This was also when he became a much-in-demand endorser for several leading products, but he always denied being fashion conscious and felt confidence and fitness could carry off anything.

If Tendulkar was seen as the ambitious middle-class man who reflected the aspirations of the people in metros in a new liberal economy in the 1990s, and Mahendra Singh Dhoni represented the aggression of those from second-tier cities during the 2000s, Kohli was the 'cool dude' that 'gen-next' looked up to in the 2010s.

The spiked-gelled hairstyle, stubble and tattoos were a hit and his aggression a major selling point. The fact that he was much younger than Tendulkar and Dhoni also ensured that his stock did not go down even when the team was not doing well post-2011 World Cup.

Yuvraj Singh, who had undergone treatment for cancer shortly after being named Man of the Series in the World Cup, and Kohli, were unscathed after the identical 4-0 Test series defeats in England and Australia. Even the 2-1 defeat at home which gave England its first Test series win in India in 28 years, did not matter.

Kohli's Adelaide century had obviously done him no harm when the team's graph was at a low and he stood rock solid in the advertising world even at a time when television viewership monitoring agency TAM Media indicated that endorsements on television by other contemporaries had fallen by more than 40 per cent!

Kohli was seen selling Fastrack watches and merchandise early on and in a matter of a few years was associated with prestigious brands like Pepsi, Nike, and Toyota. With over a dozen brands reportedly getting him a cool ₹ 3 crore each year and single-day social appearances for half that amount, the BCCI and IPL contracts paled into insignificance.

'The time that Kohli burst on to the scene was very different from what the previous generation of players like Dravid, Laxman and Kumble had experienced,' says celebrity manager Indranil Das Blah. 'Brands want to target youth in the age-group of 15-25. With his brash attitude Kohli stands for even smaller cities like Kanpur and Chandigarh.'

Blah, a partner in CAA Kwan, feels Kohli is just the right recipe when advertisers look to associate with youngsters.

'Of course, the first thing that strikes you is his performance. But he is also good-looking and speaks well. And if you are considered captaincy material that boosts one's image and demand too. He is considered a "*lambi race ka ghoda*" (one for the long run),' Blah says.

He compares Kohli with others in the Indian team and explains how he edges them out in brand endorsements: 'If you compare him to Sehwag, Kohli is better looking and more articulate; if you compare him to Gambhir, he is more consistent; if you compare him to Raina, he converses better in English. So, he is a better package overall.'

Brands want to target youth in the age-group of 15-25. With his brash attitude, Kohli stands for even smaller cities like Kanpur and Chandigarh.

It was thus no surprise that Kohli became only the

third in the ₹ 100-crore endorsements club after Tendulkar and Dhoni, within four years of playing first for the senior team, as his dependability factor kept increasing with each game.

In fact, according to data from TAM AdEX India in early 2013, Kohli had captured the second leading position with 21 per cent share of ad volumes in television media for 2012. Tendulkar led with 25 per cent while Dhoni took third spot with 15 per cent of the ad volumes.

It was no surprise then that Kohli was romantically linked with glamorous girls, including former Miss India Sarah Jane Dias and upcoming actress Tamanna. Photographs and interviews of Kohli appeared as much on the city pages, replete with parties and inaugurations, as on the sports pages.

Several awards and recognitions too boosted the Kohli brand.

He was named by the International Cricket Council as its 'One-Day Player of the Year' in September 2012, for his outstanding performance during the preceding 12 months. Kohli accrued 1,733 runs in 31 One-Day internationals at a superb average of 66.65 that included eight centuries and six half-centuries.

The BCCI's Polly Umrigar award for the 'Best Cricketer' for 2011-12 followed in November, as did the CEAT award for the same period. His performances at Adelaide, Hobart and Dhaka had obviously gone a long way in raising his profile and durability as a brand.

But Kohli is determined not to be known only as a brand and has started work on a charity foundation for underprivileged children.

'The foundation has been on my mind for a very long time. But I was going through a transition phase, so could not start off with the venture. Now, I feel it's the right time to get on with it,' he told reporters in New Delhi in March 2013.

'I know it takes time, but I think I have matured enough to start an organization for children who cannot afford an education or play any sport. If I'm able to inspire kids to achieve something, that will be my biggest achievement,' he added.

VIRAT KOHLI

Full name: Virat Prem Kohli

Born: November 5, 1988, Delhi

Style: Right-handed batsman and right-arm medium bowler

Test debut: v West Indies, Kingston, June 20, 2011, (made 4 and 15)

ODI debut: v Sri Lanka, Dambulla, August 18, 2008 (made 12)

T20I debut: v Zimbabwe, Harare, June 12, 2010 (made 26*)

CAREER STATISTICS: RUNS								
	MTS	Runs	HS	Avg	SR	100s	50s	MOM
TC	18	1175	116	41.96	46.94	4	6	1
ODI	113	4575	183	49.72	86.64	15	24	15
T20I	20	558	78*	34.87	130.37	0	4	2

TC–TEST CRICKET | MTS–MATCHES | HS–HIGHEST SCORE | SR–STRIKE RATE | MOM–MAN OF THE MATCH

Compiled by Rajnish Gupta